QUICK AND EASY THINGS YOU CAN MAKE WITH PAPER

What Quick and Easy things can you make with paper? For starters you might try a high jump apparatus, or an origami plane, or a noisemaker, or a balancing toy. This Quick and Easy guide is packed with stunts and tricks, models, toys, and designs and decorations to make.

If you follow the *blueprints,* the step-by-step directions, you can easily turn out these projects and more—such as puzzling, wacky, mixed-up pictures.

What makes these projects your very own? You add the finishing touches. You will be improving them with your own ideas and painting and decorating them just as you please. You will have finished projects that are guaranteed to be like no one else's and give you hours of fun as well.

QUICK AND EASY
THINGS YOU CAN MAKE WITH PAPER

Eric Kenneway
Illustrated by Alan Rogers

Watermill Press
Mahwah, New Jersey

Published by: **Watermill Press**
            Mahwah, N.J.

ISBN 0-8167-1682-X

Copyright © 1989 Kidsbooks, Inc.

Manufactured in the United States of America

Contents

About your assembly line

A piece of paper and a pair of scissors! Paper and scissors are practically all you need to get started on terrific paper projects.

You will use all kinds of paper—newspaper, magazine pages, thin cardboard, and tissue paper, to name just a few. In most of the projects you will be using sheets of good quality writing paper. Where the directions call for a sheet of paper, what is meant is a standard-size sheet of good quality paper, 8 ½ by 11 inches. Where other kinds of paper are needed, the instructions will clue you in.

You will need a few extra tools: a pencil, ruler, compass, and protractor and a few extra materials such as glue and paints or crayons. Use blunt scissors. Sharper scissors may sometimes be needed. Be careful when you use them. You may choose to use a penknife or craft knife, and when you do, be extra careful.

Construct your projects just like a craftsperson does—*craftily.* That means you always place your scissors pointed ends away from you; you make sure you have plenty of work space; and you use extra sheets of newspaper to protect the surfaces around you when you are painting. So line up all your materials, get your tools ready, and begin these super paper projects.

A key to the directions

1 Fold forward.

2 Fold back.

3 Cut out and do not use the shaded area.

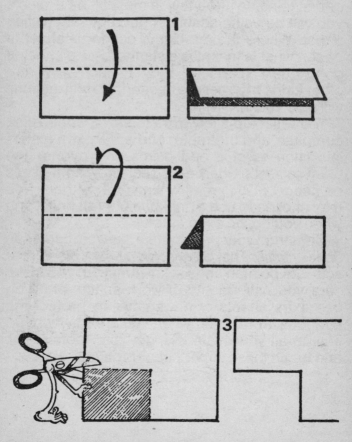

SPRINGY
SPECIALS

Jumping spiral

You will need:
one strip of paper about 1 x 10 inches

1   Curl the paper slightly by running it between your thumb and finger.

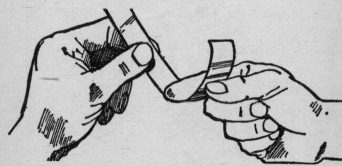

2   Then wind it into a spiral. Let the edges of the strip overlap by tiny fractions of an inch — as small as ⅛ of an inch — all the way along its length.

3   When you have finished the spiral, stand it on a table, holding it with the narrow end down. Press down into a coil and release. The spiral will jump into the air.

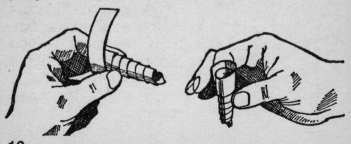

High jump apparatus

You will need:
*one sheet of thin card-
    board 8 inches long*
*one extra strip of card-
    board*
pencil and ruler
scissors
glue

You can use this apparatus to test the power of your jumping spiral. Why not match your spiral against your friends' spirals in a jumping competition?

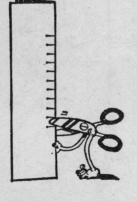

1   Cut the sheet of cardboard in half along its length. Fold one of these pieces in half where the dotted line is marked.

2   Start at a point about 2 inches from the bottom and mark ½-inch spaces up the folded edge. Then cut slits ½ inch deep at these points.

11

3   Fold the paper at each slit back at an angle, making sharp creases.

4   Push the little flaps of paper inside, between the two layers of paper. It is easier to do this if you use a stick or the point of a pair of scissors.

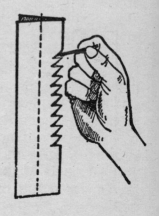

Make a crease along the dotted line by folding the left edge to the right and back. Turn over and make a similar crease on the other side.

5 Overlap the two side panels and glue them together to make a triangular tube.

Repeat steps 1 — 5, using the second piece of paper, to make another tube. These together will form the uprights of the apparatus.

6 Stand these two uprights in front of you. For the crossbar, take the extra strip of paper and fold it along its length in order to make it rigid and strong. Hang the crossbar between the uprights, resting each end on one of the little projections, or platforms.

Now measure how high your spiral will jump. When you succeed at the lower levels, raise the crossbar higher.

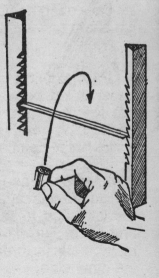

BLOWING GAMES, TOYS, AND TRICK ITEMS

Blowpipe and darts

You will need: *two sheets of paper*
pencil and ruler
scissors
tape

1   To make the pipe, roll one sheet of paper along its length to form a tube. It should measure not more than 1 inch across the end.

2   Make sure that the ends of the tube are even. Then fasten the center with a piece of tape.

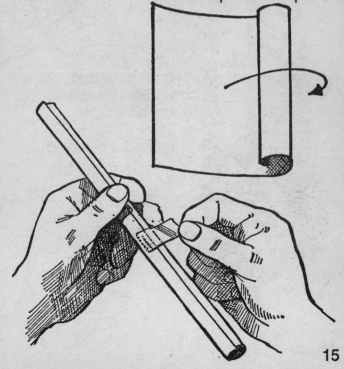

3 Next, fasten the ends with tape. This is all that is necessary to make a work-able blowpipe, but you may want to decorate it by wrapping fancy paper around it or by coloring it with felt-tipped markers.

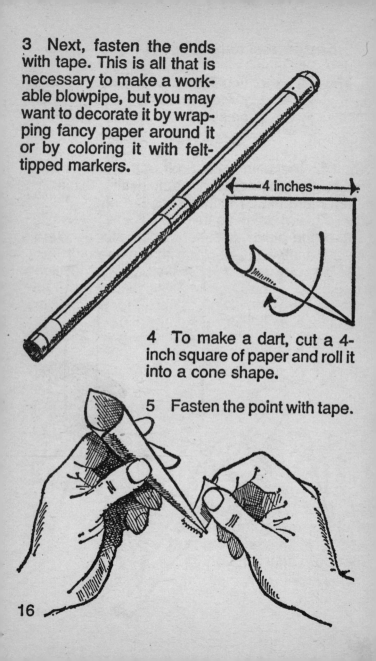

←—— 4 inches ——→

4 To make a dart, cut a 4-inch square of paper and roll it into a cone shape.

5 Fasten the point with tape.

6 Fasten the remaining edge with tape.

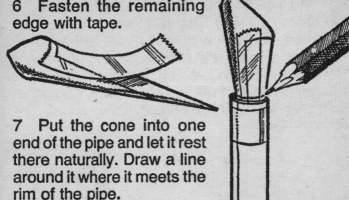

7 Put the cone into one end of the pipe and let it rest there naturally. Draw a line around it where it meets the rim of the pipe.

8 Remove the cone from the pipe and cut along the pencil line. The cone will flatten but it will spring back into shape again. Throw away the top piece.

9 Now you have a dart. Put it point first into the pipe. It should remain there and not drop right through.

10 Blow through the end into which you have just placed the dart. The dart travels with surprising force, so please do not aim it at people. A good target is a sheet of newspaper hung over a clothes line. Stand two or three yards from it and take aim. The dart will smack into the newspaper with a satisfyingly loud noise.

Screecher

You will need:
one piece of paper about 2 ½ x 4 inches
scissors

1 Fold the shorter edges of the paper together and crease.

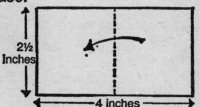

2 Cut two tiny, V-shaped pieces from the folded edge.

3 Fold the left edge to the right. Do the same behind.

4 Now let the two side pieces stand out from the middle section.

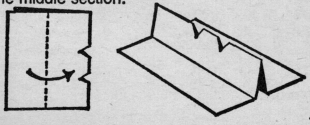

5 Hold the screecher between your first and second fingers as shown and bring it to your lips. Blow upon it, and it will produce a piercing screech.

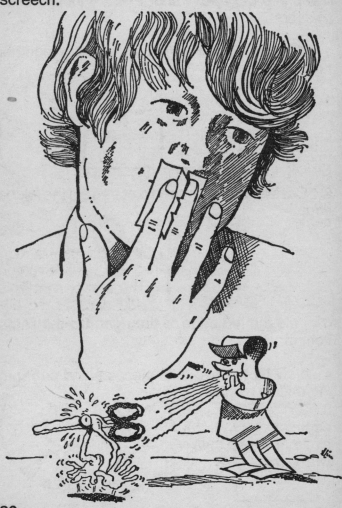

Balancing dancer

You will need: *one sheet of paper*
pencil and ruler
scissors
glue or tape
a compass
a protractor

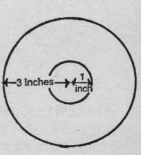

1 To make the balancing dancer's skirt, draw two circles with 1-inch and 3-inch radiuses, or measurements. Check out the drawing to see how. Then draw a horizontal line through the center of the circles.

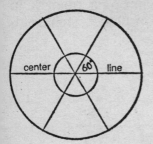

2 Using the protractor, draw 60° angles above and below the center line. This will divide each of the circles into six segments, or pieces.

3 Mark the circumference, or edge, of the outer circle at points halfway between each line.

4 Now draw a line from one of these points to the point where a nearby line cuts the inner circle. Draw five more lines, just like this one, all slanting in the same direction.

5 Cut along four of these lines. They are the dotted lines. Make further cuts as shown and throw away the shaded area.

6 Form a cone shape by bringing point X to meet point Y. Glue or tape in place. This completes the skirt.

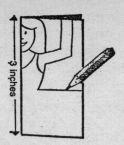

7 To make the upper body, cut a 3-inch square of paper and fold it in half. With the folded edge as the center, draw one half of a dancer with a raised arm. Draw a line from her waist to the right edge of the paper.

8 Cut through both layers along this line and around the drawing. Throw away the shaded area. Cut slits along the base.

9 Unfold and shape the lower part. Overlap the two ends and glue or tape them together.

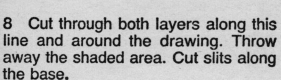
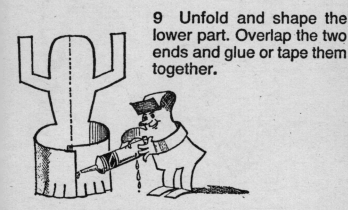

23

10 Raise the little tabs and glue them on the under side. Then place the upper body on the skirt. You may have to adjust the arms a bit.

11 Balance your dancer on the tip of a pencil. Blow her skirt, and she will spin around. You now have a balancing toy.

BOOMERANGS, TOSS AND THROW STUNT ITEMS

Boomerang cross

You will need: *one sheet of paper*
pencil and ruler
scissors

1 Start with a 3-inch square. Fold the top edge to the bottom.

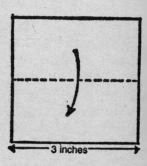

2 Fold the left edge to the right.

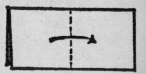

3 Measure ¼ inch in from the left and down from the top. Draw these lines. Cut along the lines through all four layers and remove the shaded area.

4 Unfold the paper and you should have the shape of a cross. Smooth out the creases.

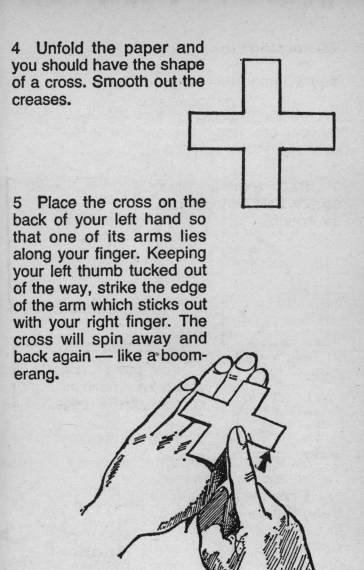

5 Place the cross on the back of your left hand so that one of its arms lies along your finger. Keeping your left thumb tucked out of the way, strike the edge of the arm which sticks out with your right finger. The cross will spin away and back again — like a boomerang.

Origami plane

You will need: *one sheet of paper*

First fold the two longer edges together, crease and open out. This is to make a center line. It is not shown in the drawings.

1 Fold the top edge to lie along the left edge.

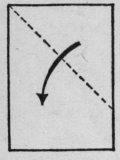 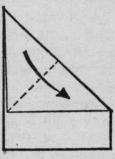

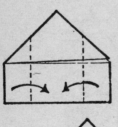

2 Fold the left edge to lie along the horizontal, or straight across, edge.

3 Fold the two sides to the center.

4 Fold the top down.   5 Fold in half behind.

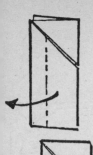

6 Fold the top flap to the left. Fold the rear flap in the same way.

7 Open out.

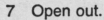

8 Launch the plane into the air, and watch it fly.

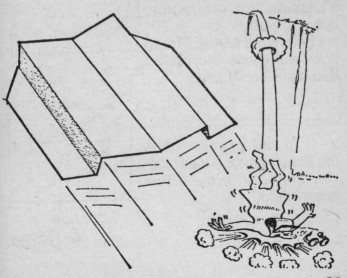

Frisbee

You will need:
one sheet of paper
pencil and ruler
scissors
a compass
a protractor

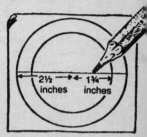

1 Draw a circle with a radius of 2½ inches. Within that circle, and using the same center point, draw a circle with a radius of 1¾ inches. Draw a horizontal line through the center.

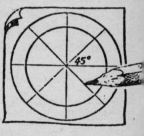

2 Using the protractor, draw a vertical line at 90⁰ and two lines at 45⁰. These lines will divide the circles into eight equal parts.

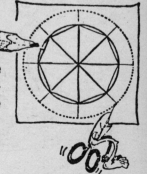

3 Join the points where the lines meet the inner circle. Then cut around the outer circle.

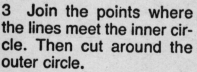

4 Cut slits along the dotted lines from the edge to the inner circle.

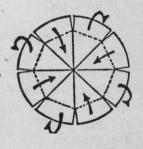

5 Fold every flap either backward or forward as shown. Let the flaps stand at sharp angles to the disc, as shown in the drawing for step 6.

6 Grip one of the flaps between your fingers. Release it by flicking your wrist forward. The frisbee will spin into the air.

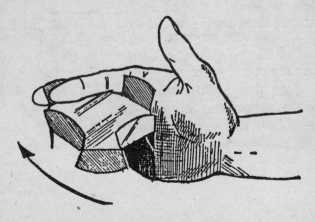

BREEZY
SPECIALS

Folding fan

You will need: *one sheet of paper at least*
12 x 20 inches
pencil, ruler, and tape

You may use pages from a magazine, but fancy wrapping paper would be better still.

1 Fold the top down on a line about 5 inches from the top edge.

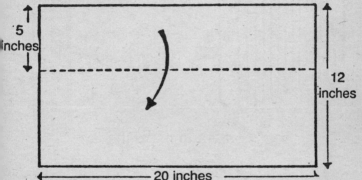

5 inches

12 inches

← 20 inches →

2 Now pleat the length of the paper into 32 sections. This can be done by first folding the paper into halves, then into quarters, into eighths, into sixteenths, and finally into 32 sections, then unfolding and pleating along these creases.

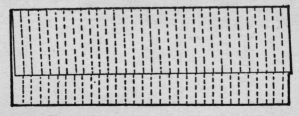

3 This is the result.

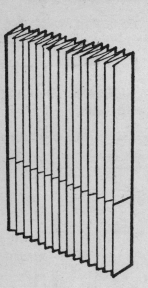

4 Form the handle by wrapping tape around the pleated paper at the 5-inch mark.

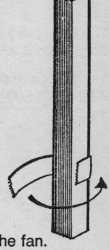

5 Open out to make the fan.

Butterflies

You will need: *one piece of colored tissue paper*
thread
a folding fan

These paper butterflies seem to come alive and dance about when they are thrown into the air.

1   Cut out a rectangle of tissue paper, about 3 x 4 inches. Twist it two or three times at the center.

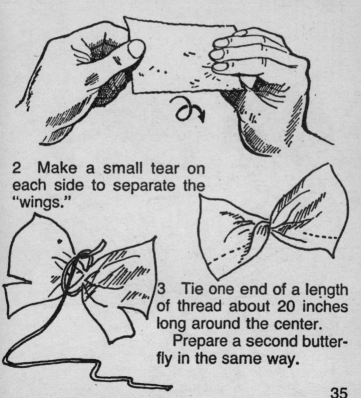

2   Make a small tear on each side to separate the "wings."

3   Tie one end of a length of thread about 20 inches long around the center.
  Prepare a second butterfly in the same way.

35

4   Take the butterflies in one hand and place the free ends of the threads in your mouth, or tie them to a button on your shirt or blouse.

Pick up the fan and release the butterflies. As you do so, fan the air beneath them. The butterflies will flutter about as if they were alive.

With experience you will discover how to keep the butterflies in the air. Sometimes long forward strokes are needed to keep the butterflies from coming too close and settling on your head or shoulders.

Pinwheel

You will need: *one sheet of paper – a magazine cover will do*
pencil and ruler
scissors
glue
a flat-headed nail about 3 inches long
a wooden stick

1   Cut an 8-inch square from the paper. Draw the two diagonal lines.

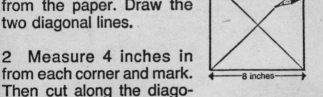

2   Measure 4 inches in from each corner and mark. Then cut along the diagonals to these points.

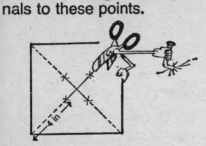

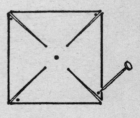

3   With the nail, make a neat hole in the center and another on each triangular flap as shown.

4 Curl one flap over so that its hole is in line with the center. Curl the three remaining flaps over in the same way.

5 Push the nail through all the holes. Work it back and forth so that it fits loosely.

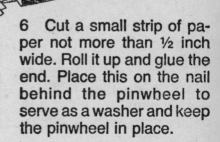

6 Cut a small strip of paper not more than ½ inch wide. Roll it up and glue the end. Place this on the nail behind the pinwheel to serve as a washer and keep the pinwheel in place.

7   Finally, push the nail into a wooden stick. Wave it in the air and the wheel will spin around. Run, and it will whirl around faster.

Rabbit in a hat

You will need: *one piece of paper 2½ x 4 inches*
pencil
glue
a toothpick

1 To make the center line, fold the two shorter edges of the paper together, crease, and open up.

 Draw a rabbit on the left and an upturned top hat on the right. Turn the paper over, keeping it the same way up.

2 Place the toothpick as shown and glue in place. Fold the left edge of the paper to the right and glue the two layers together. This makes a little banner with the rabbit on one side and the hat on the other.

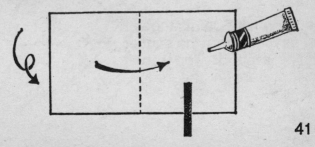

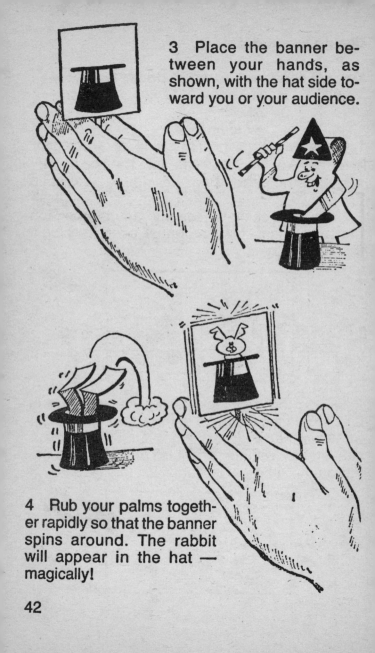

3 Place the banner between your hands, as shown, with the hat side toward you or your audience.

4 Rub your palms together rapidly so that the banner spins around. The rabbit will appear in the hat — magically!

Disappearing dot

You will need: *one scrap of paper*
felt-tipped marker or crayon
ruler

1 Draw an X on the right side of a scrap of paper.

2 Draw a dot 4 inches to the left of the X.

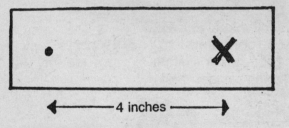

◄———— 4 inches ————►

3   Hold the paper at arm's length in front of you and look hard at the X. You will now be able to see the dot out of the corner of your eye.

4   Keep concentrating on the X and slowly bring the paper closer to your eyes. Suddenly the dot will disappear completely!

Road racing

You will need: *one large sheet of paper*
a mirror
pencil, felt-tipped marker, or
crayon

Draw big S-shaped curves on your sheet of paper. They will be your "road." Place this on a table or any other flat surface, in front of a mirror.

Point your pencil at the start of the road and look at its reflection in the mirror. With your eye on the reflection only, see if you can trace a line around the track without moving the pencil over the edge.

To make it more interesting, you can draw a track with extra twists and turns in it and surround it with hazards too, such as buildings, swamps, cliffs, and lakes.

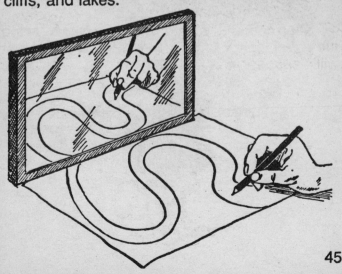

ODDS AND ENDS

Telephone

You will need: *one sheet of paper*
pencil and ruler
scissors
two empty toilet rolls
a toothpick
needle and thread – 9 yards
   or more
a compass
glue

1   Cut out a circle of paper with a radius of about 2 inches.

2   Break the toothpick neatly into two halves.

3   With the needle, pull one end of the thread through the center of the paper.

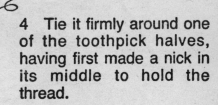

4   Tie it firmly around one of the toothpick halves, having first made a nick in its middle to hold the thread.

5 Place the paper circle, with the toothpick underneath, over the end of one of the empty toilet rolls. Make a circle of flaps around the paper by cutting from the edge of the paper to the edge of the toilet roll. You will need to hold the paper circle in place or mark it first and then cut.

6 Fold the flaps down and glue them to the roll. This completes one "handset."

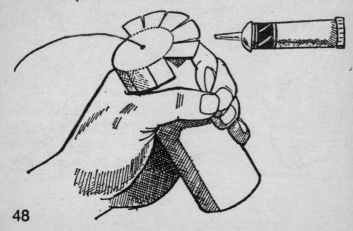

7 Repeat these steps at the other end of the thread to complete a second handset.

8 If you speak into one end of the telephone, a friend listening at the other end will be able to hear you. If you keep the thread tight, two of you will be able to carry on a conversation even when you are in separate rooms.

50

Make-believe camera

You will need: *one sheet of paper*
pencil and ruler
scissors

This little toy does not look much like a camera, but it sounds like one.

1   Cut out a rectangle of paper about 3 inches by 8 inches. Fold the two shorter edges together.

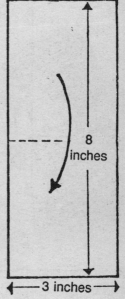

8 inches

← 3 inches →

2   Measure 1 inch from the folded top edge and 1 inch from the sides. Draw two 1½-inch lines down from these points. Cut along these lines through both layers of paper. Open up.

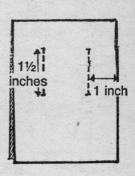

1½ inches

1 inch

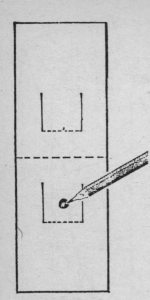

3 On the inside of the paper, cut a horizontal slit between the lower ends of each pair of vertical slits.

On the lower part, draw a circle to represent the camera lens. Then close the paper again as it was before.

4 Draw a funny face in the space framed by the cuts.

5 Separate the two layers. Push back the little flap with the face on it. Pass it underneath and behind the flap on the far side.

6 Now point your camera at a friend. Hold it as shown and pull the near side toward you. The picture will pop into view at the front with a snap!

POP-UPS
AND
TRICK PICTURES

Pop-up snake

You will need: *three or four sheets of 8 x 10 inch paper*
glue
a screw-top jar

1 Take one sheet of paper and find its center line by folding the longer edges together. Open up and fold the same two edges to the center crease. Open up again and fold the left edge over and over, as shown, to make a flat tube.

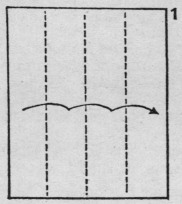

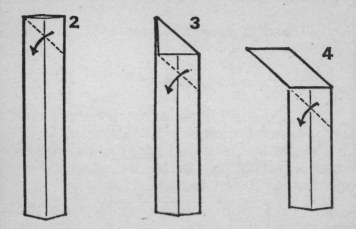

2 Fold the longer edges together to find the center line. Open up and fold the top edge so that it lies along the left edge.

3 Now fold the horizontal edge to the left edge.

4 Do this again, until you make the shape illustrated in drawing 5. Then open up.

56

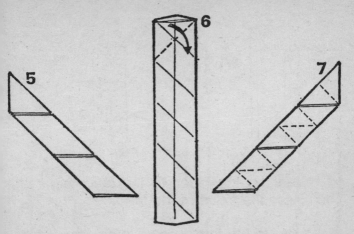

5, 6, and 7   You now have a series of equally spaced, diagonal creases running down the paper. Make a second series to cross the first. Start by folding the top edge to the right edge and continue in the same way until the shape illustrated in drawing 7 is made. Then open up.

8 and 9   Make a series of equally spaced horizontal creases by pleating. See drawing 9. Then open up.

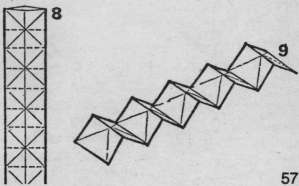

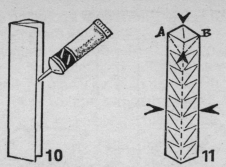

10 Glue the top layer to the layer beneath. Then raise the sides of the tube.

11 Now start to form accordion folds using the creases which are already in place. First push in the two top V-like sections and then flatten the tube (it helps to insert a ruler). Points A and B can now be pinched into a horizontal position.

12 Squeeze the sides to re-form the tube and immediately flatten the other way. Watch point X.

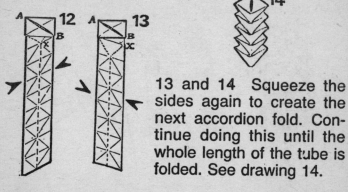

13 and 14 Squeeze the sides again to create the next accordion fold. Continue doing this until the whole length of the tube is folded. See drawing 14.

15 Make two or three more accordion sections as shown in steps 1-14 and link them together by raising two points at the end of one section and placing them into the two "pockets" of another section. A spot of glue will help to hold them together. This forms your snake.

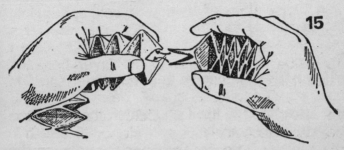

16 Finish by drawing the snake's eyes. A small scrap of paper will make a tongue. Pack the snake neatly into a jar. When the top is removed, the snake will pop out.

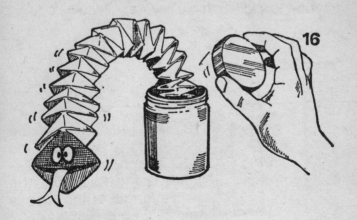

Flexagon

You will need: *two sections of the pop-up snake made from 8 x 10 inch sheets of fancy wrapping paper*

Join two sections of the pop-up snake, then join the two ends together in the same way. This makes a sort of doughnut shape which is called a flexagon.

Push the sides down and the center spreads outward, changing its shape. Keep on twisting the flexagon into itself and watch the changing pattern of its surfaces.

Magic pictures

You will need: *paper 3 x 4 inches in size*
pencil and ruler
scissors
tape
glue
magazine pictures to cut out

1 Mark every inch along the edges of the paper. Join the points together to divide the sheet into twelve 1-inch squares. Then mark each square with a number as shown. Turn the paper over, keeping it the same way up.

2 Divide the other side into twelve squares and number as shown.

1	1	2	3
3	2	1	1
1	1	2	3

↶

4	4	3	2
2	3	4	4
4	4	3	2

← 3 inches →

← 4 inches →

4	4	3	2
2	3	4	4
4	4	3	2

3 Now cut neatly along the broken line to make a rectangular flap. Fold this to the right.

4 Fold the left edge of the paper to the center...

5 ...and fold again.

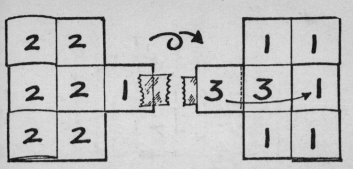

6   Stick a piece of tape on the end of the projecting flap. Turn over...

7   ...and fold the flap to the right, fixing it firmly to the square behind the window.

8   The basic construction is now finished.
You will notice that the front surface has six squares each marked with a **1**. Fold in half from right to left.

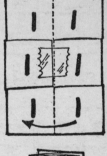

9   Separate the two layers at the right...

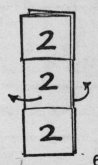

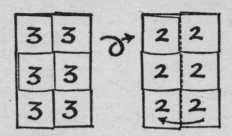

10 ...and the new surface is marked with **3**s. Turn over.

11 This surface is marked with **2**s. Fold in half from right to left.

12 Separate the layers at the right again.

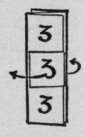

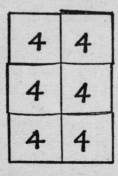

13 You now have a complete set of **4**s.

14 Cut a set of four pictures of the right size from a magazine. Trim them into 3-inch by 2-inch rectangles. Call the pictures number **1**, number **2**, etc. Cut picture number **1** into six 1-inch squares. Return the toy to the position in which all the **1**s can be seen, and carefully stick each piece of picture number **1** into its square so that the complete picture is reassembled. Do the same with the other three pictures.

Now hand your magic picture puzzle to a friend and ask your friend to find the hidden pictures!

More magic pictures

You will need: *drawing paper*
pencil and ruler
scissors
glue

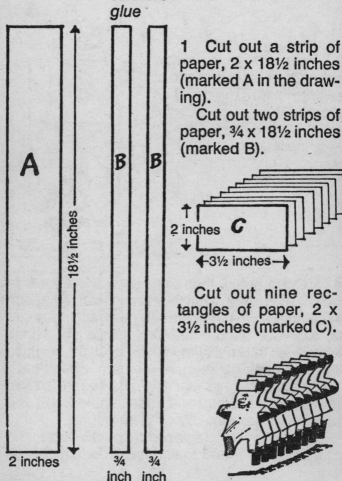

1 Cut out a strip of paper, 2 x 18½ inches (marked A in the drawing).

Cut out two strips of paper, ¾ x 18½ inches (marked B).

Cut out nine rectangles of paper, 2 x 3½ inches (marked C).

2 Take the two narrow strips B and glue one end of each to one rectangle C as shown. Make sure that the edges of the strips line up with the edges of the rectangle. Then turn over.

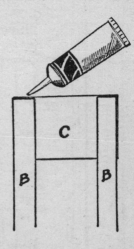

3 Glue strip A to the other side of the rectangle, making sure that the top edges of both are even. Strip A should lie exactly between strips B.

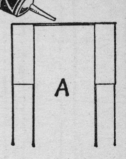

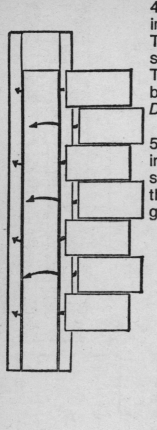

4 Now weave the remaining rectangles into position. The first one should lie over strips B but under strip A. The next one under strips B but over strip A, and so on. *Do not glue.*

5 Slip the final rectangle into place. This is one you should glue in the way that the first rectangle was glued.

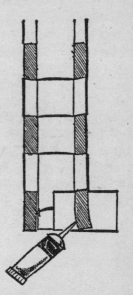

6 You now have a chain of nine squares. Draw a series of pictures, one on each square except for the end squares. You might use pictures cut from a magazine if you prefer.

Then pleat the whole thing, neatly folding backward and forward on the lines shown.

7 This makes a folder of pictures ready to show to your friends. Raise the first layer, as if you were opening a book. Lift it, and let the folder fall open naturally. There are the pictures you drew — as you would expect.

8 Close the folder again. This time turn the magic pictures around or take the opposite end, and let the folder fall open. It takes a bit of experimenting.

9 The pictures have disappeared!

FRICTION
ITEMS

Mary and her little lamb

You will need: *one sheet of paper*
pencil and ruler
scissors
glue or tape
felt-tipped pens or crayons)s

1   To make Mary, fold the two shorter edges of the paper together and crease firmly. Draw one half of a girl centered on the folded edge. Draw a horizontal line from the girl to the right edge, below the center. Cut along this line through both layers and around the outline of the drawing above it. Remove the shaded area carefully.

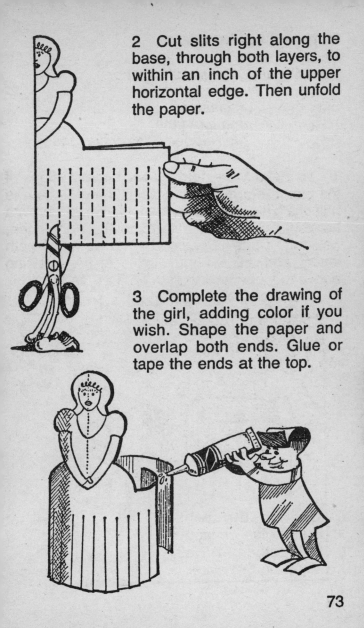

2 Cut slits right along the base, through both layers, to within an inch of the upper horizontal edge. Then unfold the paper.

3 Complete the drawing of the girl, adding color if you wish. Shape the paper and overlap both ends. Glue or tape the ends at the top.

4 To make the little lamb, take a small piece of paper and fold it in half. Draw this shape and cut around it. Remove the shaded area.

5 Cut slits along the base. Bring the head down. Turn it inside out and pinch it into position.

6 Overlap the two ends and glue or tape them together at the top. Draw in the eyes.

7   Place Mary and her lamb on top of an upturned cardboard box. Tap gently and Mary will run forward with the little lamb following.

Other subjects can be treated in this way.

You could have a whole flock of animals. The larger figure could be a Noah. In that case you would have a Noah's Ark!

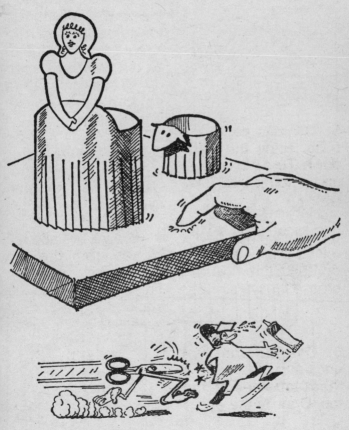

Beetle race

You will need: *one sheet of paper*
one extra 2-inch square of colored paper
pencil and ruler
scissors

1 To make a track for the beetle, fold the two longer edges of the sheet of paper together, crease, and open up. Cut this crease line up to about 2 inches from the top.

2 Fold the two sides to the center line. Crease firmly and turn over.

3 Bring the two folded edges to the center line and crease firmly.

4 Draw a line about 2 inches from the top (where the cut ends). This completes the track.

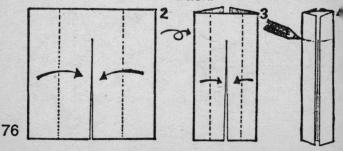

5 To make the beetle, fold opposite sides of the little square of colored paper together in turn and leave folded in half.

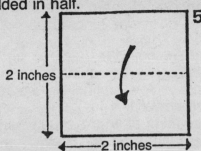

6 Make sure the folded edge is at the top. Then fold the top right corner to center bottom. Turn over.

7 Fold the top right corner to center bottom.

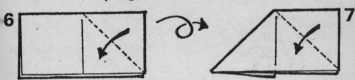

8 Now pull the middle layers apart, opening out the center. Allow the two sides to flatten out and the corners to come together in the center.

9 This is the beetle completed.

10 Slide the beetle onto the track. Each triangular flap of the beetle should run either above or below one of the two top, folded edges of the track.

11 To operate, hold the track as shown and make it rustle slightly by moving each hand back and forth rapidly. You will find that the beetle will start to move upward.

Shift the position of your hands when necessary, moving them up the track behind the beetle, but not touching it.

Get your friends to make beetles and tracks too so that you can have beetle races.

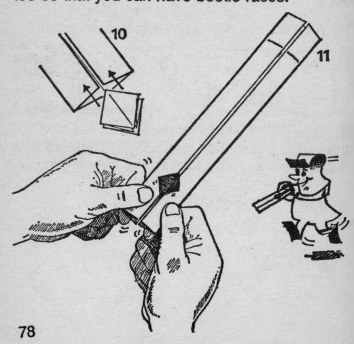

DESIGNS
AND
DECORATIONS

Totem pole

You will need: *one sheet of paper or thin cardboard*
scissors

Cut the sheet of paper into four quarters.

1   Take one of the four pieces and fold two edges together, either along the length or width.

2   Treating the folded edge as the center, make cuts through the two layers of paper to create a strange mask. Cut a mouth, nose, eyes and ears, strange horns, tusks, wrinkles in the forehead, and lines in the cheeks. Throw away the shaded areas. Let your imagination be your guide. You can make all sorts of masks. No two need be alike. You can make larger masks and masks from colored paper as well.

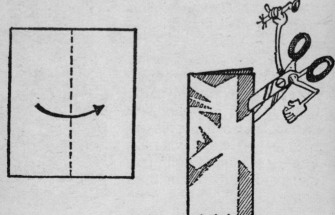

3   Cut a small, vertical slit through both layers at the top of the mask. Make more masks from the remaining three pieces of paper. Fold some of the pieces along the width and some along the length so that your masks are not all of the same height and width.

4   Using the slits, slot the masks into each other to form a totem pole. By using more sheets of paper you can build up the pole as high as you like. If you plan a really tall totem pole, use thin cardboard rather than paper.

All kinds of cut-outs

You will need: *squares of paper (start with news-paper and then try other kinds of paper)*
scissors

Fold the square of paper in half.

1 Fold the top layer of the bottom edge up to the folded edge. Turn over and do the same to the other side.

2 Fold the right edge to the left edge.

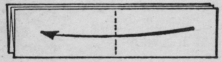

3 Fold the top layer of the left edge to the folded edge. Turn over and do the same to the other side.

This gives you a little square of paper of sixteen layers. By cutting into this shape and unfolding, you can discover many interesting patterns.

4 Simply cutting away each corner of the little square, for example, creates a grid pattern.

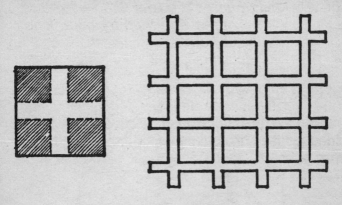

5 By cutting these two curves you will have a fascinating pattern.

Experiment, and when you find a pattern which you like, repeat it and make several cut-outs of the same pattern. You can use the cut-outs to decorate the cover of a book or a part of a wall.

Six-pointed snowflake patterns

You will need: *squares of paper – newspaper will do*
scissors

1 Take one square of paper and fold two opposite points together to make a crease. Open up again. Fold the other two points together and leave them folded.

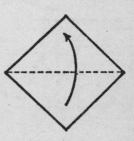

2 Making sure that the creases start from the center of the folded edge, bring the two side points forward to lie across each other.

3 Carefully pull the points apart so that the angle where the edges of the two flaps meet (point X) is in line with the other center crease. Now crease firmly.

4 Fold in half from right to left.

5 Make cuts through all layers, throwing away the shaded area, and unfold.

6 You have finished a six-pointed snowflake pattern. Now that you know how, try other kinds of paper. You could hang your snowflakes. A group of them make an interesting mobile.

Five-pointed stars

You will need: *squares of paper – again, news-paper will do to start you off scissors*

There is a bit of a mystery in creating a regular five-pointed shape just by fold-ing and cutting a four-sided sheet of paper. So, even though it is easier to make four-pointed or eight-point-ed shapes, you may want to tackle these more mysteri-ous five-pointed ones. Here is one way of doing it.

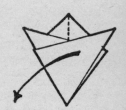

1   Fold a square of paper into the shape shown on page 84. Then bring the flap down.

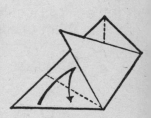

2   Fold the bottom edge to the diagonal edge as shown. Make a crease and open flat again.

3   Now re-position the tri-angular flap so that its lower edge lies along the crease made in the previous step.

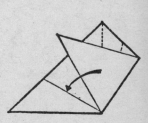

4 Fold the flap in half.

 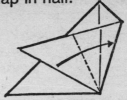

5 Fold the left point across the folded edge.

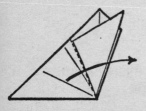 

6 Fold the point to the left.

7 This is the shape ready for cutting.

8 By making one cut like this, you create a simple, five-pointed star shape.

9 By making more cuts like this, you create several overlaid star shapes.

Five-petalled flowers

1 Cutting a curved line into the shape shown on page 87 produces a simple flower.

2 Extra cuts produce combined petal and leaf shapes. Experiment with cutting shapes of this kind. Try overlapping two or three shapes to get even more spectacular results.

Cut-out patterns such as these can be made from small or large squares of paper. Small patterns are useful for decorating envelopes or for making greeting cards. They can be glued to folded sheets of paper to make cards.

Much larger cut-outs can be made into a wall-sized decoration for your room.

89

Honeycomb paper ball

You will need: *one old magazine about 10 x 12 inches*
cardboard
pencil and ruler
scissors
a compass
glue and tape
a toothpick

1   Prepare sixty rectangles of paper, about 4 x 7 inches. To do this quickly, tear twenty pages from a magazine, then cut the batch of pages into thirds, cutting across the width of the pages. Reduce the longer side to 7 inches by trimming the paper.

Overlap the sheets so that a little of each is showing along the longer side. Measure off at 1½-inch spaces from the left short edge. The last interval will be only 1 inch. Draw lines at this point so that each sheet is marked.

You may not be able to mark all of the sheets together in this way. Work with batches of paper that you can handle most comfortably.

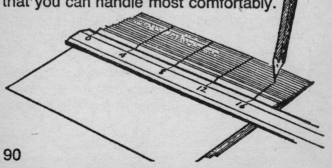

2   Take one sheet and run a line of glue first along the left edge. (Use a toothpick unless your glue has a thin nozzle attachment.) Run other lines of glue across the sheet from each of the 1½-inch marks.

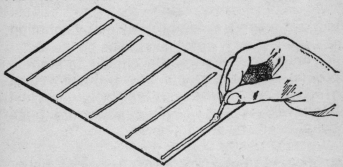

3   Take a second sheet and *turn it around so that the 1-inch mark is at the left.* Now lay it on top of the first sheet. Run a line of glue along the right edge and then across from each mark.

Continue sticking the sheets together, remembering to turn every second sheet around, so that the lines of glue between them alternate like bricks in a wall.

3½ inches or slightly smaller

4 - When all sixty sheets are glued together, draw a circle with a 3½-inch radius on the folded cardboard. Cut out the half-circle and then cut along its fold so that you have two half-circles.

Place one of these half-circles on the glued sheets, edge to edge, and cut through the sheets around it.

5 Glue the half-circle of cardboard to the top and bottom sheets of magazine paper. Then stick tape along the spine to make a "book."

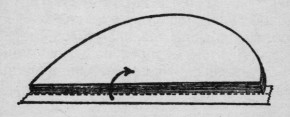

6   Open up the "book" and the sheets will separate into a honeycomb design. Bring the two covers together behind and the decoration will take the form of a ball. Fasten with tape so that the ball will keep its form, and hang it up. Lots of honeycombs make super party decorations.

More honeycomb decorations

Instead of using two half-circles of cardboard as described on page 92, cut other shapes to produce many kinds of honeycomb forms.

The bell decoration is put together in the same way as the ball, except that two half-bell shapes are used instead of half-circles. The Christmas tree combines two simple shapes joined by a strip of cardboard. The fish is made from two half-opened oval forms, glued back to back, with cardboard shapes added for the fins and tail.

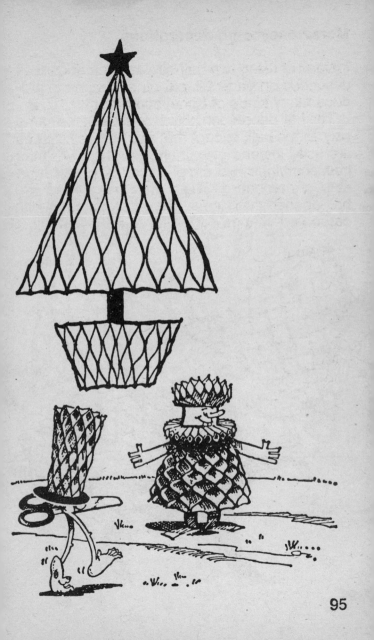